To

From

LEGACIES

Children Celebrate Their Grandmothers

Compiled by Sally & Libbey Koppinger

papier-mache ®

Papier-Mache Press
Watsonville, CA

Copyright © 1998 by Sally A. Koppinger and Elizabeth A. Koppinger. Printed in the United States of America. All rights reserved including the right to reproduce this book or portions thereof in any form. For information contact Papier-Mache Press, 627 Walker Street, Watsonville, CA 95076.

02 01 00 99 98   5 4 3 2 1

ISBN: 1-57601-058-9 Softcover

Cover and interior design by Libbey Koppinger
Copyediting by Shirley Coe
Authors photograph by Rick Luettke
Manufactured by Vaughan Printing

Library of Congress Cataloging-in-Publication Data

Legacies: children celebrate their grandmothers / compiled by Sally & Libbey Koppinger;
  (together with the children of St. Joseph School).
        p.   cm.
     ISBN 1-57601-058-9 (pbk. : acid free- recycled paper)
     1. Grandmothers -- Miscellanea. 2. Grandparent and child - Miscellanea.
   3. Conduct of life -- Miscellanea. I. Koppinger, Sally, 1942 -   .
   II. Koppinger, Libbey, 1965 -   . III. St. Joseph School (Sylvania, Ohio)
   HQ759.9.L43 1998
   306.874'5-dc21   97-41157
                                                               CIP

I n t r o d u c t i o n

When Libbey wrote *Legacy: Gifts from a Grandmother* a few years ago, our family received a genuine outpouring from people we knew well and from others we didn't know at all. They told us about their families, even sharing grammaisms—gentle lessons and simple wisdom — from their own grandmothers. We were pleased so many people connected with *Legacy*.

We knew that Therese VanWormer (Libbey's grandmother and Sally's mother), for whom the original book was written, would have loved that all the gifts of wisdom and laughter she left to her family were being shared with and enjoyed by so many people. *Share*. That was perhaps one of her best messages to us. Gramma/Mom had a way of getting right down to the point. We didn't realize, however, what a universal trait that was among grandmothers until Sally received a very special gift.

Sally is the principal of St. Joseph School in Sylvania, Ohio. As a birthday present last year, the teachers at St. Joe's asked each of their students to think about their own grammas and write down one thing their grammas always said or one thing they had learned from their gramma. Those gramma-isms, over 700 of them, were compiled into a huge poster board-sized book and presented to Sally.

After reading and rereading this wonderful gift, we decided, together with the children and teachers at St. Joseph School, that these new gramma-isms ought to be shared. The result is this little book—a heartfelt, soulful, and often humorous look at how profoundly our grandmothers touch our lives, even in our earliest years.

These children echo the very best messages to be passed from generation to generation. They remind us that life is both precious and fun. Here we read that our grandmothers remain with us—at playtime, in kitchens baking cookies, on long-distance phone calls, in the stories they've told us, when making sure we don't spoil our appetites, as they kiss away our hurts...

Our grandmothers teach us about life—both the practical and profound, the silly and serious. And we learn that no matter how old we are, our grammas stay in our hearts forever.

—*Sally & Libbey Koppinger*

Dedicated to the memory of Therese C. VanWormer

How precious you are to us
for your loveliness,
your wisdom,
your laughter, your love.

Kindergarten

I love grammo

k i n d e r g a r t e n

Always keep your room clean. ~ *Trevor*

Never hold a grudge. ~ *Abby & Anne*

Keep peace in your heart and have a happy spirit. ~ *Ben & Emily*

You are a real angel. ~ *Hilary*

Look beyond the stars. ~ *Taylor*

Have faith in the unknown. ~ *Andrew*

Take pride in yourself. ~ *Brooke & Paige*

There's no one else like you. ~ *Jessica*

k i n d e r g a r t e n

You bring me happiness. ~ *Brittanie & Aaron*

Always try your best. ~ *Drake, Matt, & Christopher*

Put on a happy face! ~ *Cody, Jonathan, & Ryan*

Try to make others happy. ~ *Chris, Erin, Danielle, & Andrew*

I'm glad you've come to visit. ~ *Nick & Nicholas*

I miss you every moment you're away. ~ *Dean*

Say you're sorry when you hurt someone's feelings.
~ *Jennifer, Evan, & Kaylee*

k   i   n   d   e   r   g   a   r   t   e   n

Include everyone when you play. ~ *Emily & Eric*

Play fair. ~ *Joe, Kevin, Libby, & Douglas*

Be willing to take turns! ~ *Tom, John, & Elizabeth*

Help others in need. ~ *Olivia, Zachary, & Molly*

Be open and honest. ~ *Nile*

Love everyone. ~ *Grace, Marie, & Julianne*

Enjoy life to the fullest. ~ *Jessica*

Kiss and hug Mom and Dad every day. ~ *Matthew*

Tell your parents you love them. ~ *Kelsey & Brian*

Ask before you go in the candy room. ~ *Matthew*

Brush your teeth in the night. ~ *Kyle & A.J.*

Go to bed when you are told. ~ *Morgan, Eric, & Alexandra*

Put away your paper dolls when you are done. ~ *Allison*

Gramma didn't get mad when I picked all the flowers
in her yard. ~ *Elizabeth*

k i n d e r g a r t e n

You only need two drops of soap to wash the dishes. ~ *Abbie*

Save your rocks because they are
something special from your childhood. ~ *Cory*

Be quiet around your sleeping baby brother. ~ *Kelly*

Use your napkin when your hands get dirty. ~ *Julie & Tess*

Say your prayers before you go to bed. ~ *Travis*

Finish your bowl of cereal. ~ *Lindsay*

Gramma taught me how to sew a gift. ~ *Elizabeth*

k i n d e r g a r t e n

Put your trucks away in the corner. ~ *Zachary*

Lift the clouds of hate and fear. ~ *Jack*

Don't take too many Go Fish cards! ~ *Danny*

Make sure you say please and thank-you. ~ *Elisha & Krystyn*

When you are in the store, always hang onto the cart. ~ *Lauren*

Try to color on the paper. ~ *Steven*

Share and play together. ~ *Patrick, Taylor, & Samantha*

Don't go too close to a fire. ~ *Kayla*

Swim with a grown-up. *~ Katie*

Play nice. *~ Kelly, Ross, Scott, & Kelsey*

Look out for the other persons. *~ Max & Juleigh*

Keep friends by being friendly. *~ Elizabeth & Ashley*

Thank God for each new day. *~ Kathryn*

Life is worth living. *~ Joseph*

I think you're special. *~ Alex & Bryan*

First Grade

Always zip your coat. ~ *Ashley*

Don't eat too much sugar. ~ *Matt*

Don't fall in the snow. ~ *Adam*

I'll love you forever! ~ *Ashley, Nick, & Devin*

Always say a thank-you. ~ *Sean & Joey*

Gramma taught me to count. ~ *Nicole*

Gramma taught me to open cans of pop safely. ~ *Timmy*

Gramma taught me to play croquet. ~ *Ross*

Always take a cookie from the jar! ~ *Kim*

It's not how fast you do your work, but how nice. ~ *Melanie*

When you are in a crowd, stick together! ~ *Tony*

I'll always be your gramma. ~ *Bradley & Ben*

Be careful when fishing *not* to fall in the water. ~ *Dan*

Gramma taught me to play checkers. ~ *Brian*

Gramma taught me to write my name. ~ *Brett*

Gramma taught me how to flip pancakes and bake cookies and brownies. ~ *Mitchell, Courtney, & Megan*

Never yell in the house; use your "inside" voice!
~ *Thomas & Monica*

Be kind to your brothers and sisters ~ *Sarah & Andy*

Always take your time with your schoolwork. ~ *Ian & Mike*

Look before you cross the street. ~ *Andy & Bethany*

Gramma always takes me to the store. ~ *Angela*

Gramma taught me to play spoons on my knee. ~ *Andy*

Gramma taught me how to play football! ~ *Brian*

Always wave good-bye. ~ *Cameron*

Never run in the hall at school. ~ *Brendan*

I'll always be with you. ~ *Katie, Michelle, & Kelsie*

Love each other. ~ *Nicole & Adam*

Sometimes the oldest tricks work the best. ~ *James*

Gramma makes me scrambled eggs. ~ *Kellie*

Gramma taught me how to play chopsticks on her piano. ~ *Sam*

Gramma taught me how to sew. ~ *Brooke & Laura*

Always remember to wipe your feet at the door! ~ *Steven*

How much you've grown! ~ *Jennifer*

Wait to have sugar or candy till *after* dinner.
~ *Kevin, Brittany, & Dane*

Play cats cradle with yarn. ~ *Kristen*

Gramma makes the best turkey. ~ *Madeline*

Gramma likes to take me to K-mart. ~ *Alexandria*

Gramma taught me to write stories. ~ *Rachael*

Don't eat all of the cookie dough when you bake. ~ *Zachary*

Always chew with your mouth closed. ~ *Mike*

Say "Hi" to all your neighbors. ~ *Chelsea*

Yes you can. ~ *Matt*

Gramma taught me how to cook a grilled cheese sandwich
and how to cook eggs. ~ *Alyssa & Emily*

Gramma taught me how to put together a
5,000-piece puzzle. ~ *Valerie*

Gramma taught me to use chopsticks. ~ *Danielle*

f i r s t   g r a d e

Just one more. ~ *Steven*

Always say your prayers before bed. ~ *Megan*

Whatever your heart desires! ~ *Kathleen*

(When I spend the night with her.)
Go to bed! ~ *Amanda*

Gramma plays baby bear with my little sister and me. ~ *Nicole*

Gramma taught me to read. ~ *Jeff*

Gramma taught me to hunt. ~ *Alex*

first grade

Okeydokey! ~ *Kathleen*

Don't drink lying down. ~ *Glenn*

Don't stay up too late. ~ *Allison*

I love you with all my heart. ~ *Luke*

Be gentle when holding fragile things. ~ *Abigail*

Gramma puts a cold cloth on my head when I'm hot. ~ *Christopher*

We walk and talk together. ~ *Owen & Lauren*

Gramma takes me to the toy store. ~ *Michael, Jack, & Christopher*

Remember to feed the fish! ~ *Aaron*

I love you. ~ *James & Elizabeth*

Put on your coat before you go outside. ~ *Kathryn*

(To my grandpa.) Wake up! ~ *Corey*

Gramma says "Hi" to me first, and then talks to my mom ~ *John*

We watch movies together at her house. ~ *Andrew*

Gramma taught me to swim. ~ *Kyle & Max*

Gramma taught me how to stay with her in a store. ~ *Caitlin*

Second Grade

Oh, my you're growing. ~ *Joey, Kathryn, & Eamon*

You're almost as tall as me! ~ *Hank*

Drink all your milk after you eat your cereal. ~ *Meaghan*

Your sewing is getting better! ~ *Bailey*

Stay at the table after you're finished eating. ~ *Meghan*

Study hard to make it into Notre Dame. ~ *Nick*

Be quiet in church. ~ *Rollin*

Gramma lets me help make peanut butter cookies. ~ *Stephanie*

Don't be bored! ~ *Kerrie*

Work hard in school. ~ *Matt*

Always chew with your mouth closed. ~ *Erin*

Hi ya, honey, how're you doing? ~ *Tyler*

I love you. ~ *Caitlin*

Try your best in everything. ~ *Michael & Emily*

Be a good listener. ~ *Danyelle*

Gramma likes to play games and cards with me. ~ *Sarah-Jo & Sean*

You are special the way you are. ~ *Kristen & Lindsay*

No fighting. ~ *Paul & Patrick*

Don't sit too close to the TV. ~ *Cristin*

Don't say bad words. ~ *Chip*

Don't get too close to the fire. ~ *Mark*

Have a good day. ~ *Nick*

Gramma loves to read to me
and tells great stories. ~ *Erin, Lauren, & Steven*

s e c o n d g r a d e

Go to bed on time. ~ *Stephanie*

Always brush your teeth and wash your face before you go to bed.
~ *Leah, Elisabeth, & Sonny*

You never get too spoiled at Gramma's. ~ *Danny*

Stay away from the ironing board when the iron is hot. ~ *Allan*

Always be kind to your brother. ~ *Allison, Megan, & Monica*

Do your best in art. ~ *Kevin*

Always say your prayers at night. ~ *Melissa*

Gramma taught me to play nice with her dog. ~ *Kelly*

Do your best in school. ~ *A.J. & Forrest*

Believe in yourself and always tell the truth. ~ *Tom & Claire*

Read as many books as you can. ~ *Alexandra*

Do your homework the best you can. ~ *Erika*

What are you going to be when you grow up? ~ *Greg & Chris*

Always forgive your sisters. ~ *Lindsey*

Sticks and stones may break my bones
but words will never hurt me ~ *Olivia*

Gramma taught me to draw 3-D art. ~ *Kelsey*

Be good to your sisters. ~ *Sara & Brandon*

If you keep reading, you'll get very smart. ~ *Emily*

Don't be scared, because Jesus is always with you. ~ *David*

Don't reach across the table. ~ *Sarah*

Stay in bed when you're sick. ~ *Rachel*

Never hurt your friends. ~ *Brian*

Remember to feed the dog before he eats your dinner! ~ *Robby*

Gramma plays checkers with me. ~ *Maemee*

s e c o n d g r a d e

Don't be late for dinner. ~ *Michael*

Treat others the way you want to be treated. ~ *David & Stephan*

Don't touch the stove. ~ *Nicholas*

Make good choices. ~ *Stephanie, Jim, & Marc*

It doesn't matter if you're first or last, as long as you try. ~ *Tim*

Curve your fingers when you play the piano. ~ *Christine*

Don't get mad if you can't "get it." ~ *Joe*

Gramma taught me to make pudding. ~ *Tim*

Don't be mean to the dog. ~ *Amanda*

Say please and thank-you. ~ *Alison & Molly*

Never run in front of the car. ~ *Marianne*

Don't be a tattletale. ~ *Greg*

Be nice to people you don't like. ~ *Meredith*

Never let down your friends. ~ *Tommy*

Don't hit or jump on the cat. ~ *Nicole*

Gramma always lets me help her. ~ *Shane*

Make good choices. ~ *Jim*

Never give up. ~ *Ronnie*

Try your hardest. ~ *Mary & Michael*

Don't kick people. ~ *Matt*

Don't play in the mud. ~ *Lindsey*

Always love Jesus. ~ *Kathryn*

Gramma taught me to tie-dye shirts! ~ *Devon*

Gramma loves to hug and kiss me. ~ *Anthony*

Third Grade

Don't leave food for the giant. ~ *Alex*

Always eat your vegetables before dessert.
~ *Katie, Julie, Kristie, & Kirsten*

Come in and wipe off your feet. ~ *Erin & Patrick*

Wash your hands before you eat.
~ *Lauren, Brad, Ashley, & Brittany*

Read a book, *now!* ~ *Jennifer*

Think before you act. ~ *Brendan*

Always wear your coat.
~ *Kate, Ryan, Joey, Angelique, & Chris*

I love you. ~ *Kristen*

Don't be a hog! ~ *Jason*

Put your socks on or you will catch cold. ~ *Lizzie*

Go to the bathroom before you go to bed. ~ *Ben*

Don't fight with your sister. ~ *Michael*

Clean your room or bugs, rats, and mice will get in! ~ *Chris*

Stop sleeping and do something! ~ *Stephen*

Clear off your dish before you go outside. ~ *Joey*

Always wash your hands after touching the dog. ~ *Emily*

Eat what you want. ~ *Katie*

Don't play with the bell. ~ *John*

Spend your money wisely. ~ *Miranda*

Curiosity killed the cat. ~ *Patrick*

Make your bed and wash your hands. ~ *Kathryn*

Eat *all* your food or no dessert! ~ *Molly*

Go play with your brother and sister. ~ *Kaitlin*

Always wash your hands before dinner. ~ *John*

If Mom says no, ask Gramma. ~ *Betsy*

Take your medicine well. ~ *Mark*

Use every opportunity to win. ~ *Mary*

Never cross the street without looking first. ~ *JoAnna*

Don't touch electric wires. ~ *Sundeep*

Always use light strokes
when making a mountain with paint. ~ *Tyler*

Chew before you swallow. ~ *John*

Give your grandchildren chocolate milk in their bottles. ~ *Tom*

Greet people you know. ~ *Erin*

Don't let your brother into your room when he's furious. ~ *Katie*

Always wipe your feet when you come in. ~ *Anthony*

Do not wear anyone else's glasses. ~ *Blaize*

Always be kind to others. *~ Amy*

Wear slippers so you don't catch cold. *~ Daniel*

Stay away from your brother when he's mad. *~ Lauren*

Cut down your Christmas tree. *~ Matthew*

Don't get into a stranger's car. *~ Thea*

Never cheat. *~ Alan*

Always wash your hands after you go to the bathroom. *~ Clay*

Don't smoke because you can die, and you can get sick. *~ Aaron*

Chew with your mouth closed. ~ *Grace*

Help out. ~ *Patrick*

Always color in the lines. ~ *Jillian*

Decorate in peach and pink. ~ *Danielle*

Try to do your best at everything. ~ *Sarah*

Be polite and share with others. ~ *Kyle*

Don't pick your nose. ~ *Nathan*

Always love your family. ~ *Christie*

Eat everything on your plate. ~ *Billy*

Brush your teeth after every meal. ~ *Stephanie*

Only walk to the park with me. ~ *Emily*

Always taste food before you say it's bad. ~ *Ryan*

Don't eat too much candy in one day. ~ *Adam*

Always wash behind your ears. ~ *Kitty*

Never give up; keep trying. ~ *Greg*

Do not boss people around! ~ *Samantha*

Always wear clean clothes at special occasions. ~ *Eric*

No sweets before dinner, lunch, and breakfast. ~ *Bart*

Don't stand too close to the marsh. ~ *Mary*

Play the computer after school. ~ *Kelly*

If it doesn't taste good, don't eat it. ~ *David*

Always be a little early. ~ *Mark*

Don't mess around in the house. ~ *Matt*

Never believe your grandpa. ~ *Mark*

Put a Band-Aid on a blister. ~ *Alyssa*

Take your gum out before you go to bed. ~ *Jenna*

Do not eat beans at someone else's party. ~ *Phil*

Never start to smoke. ~ *Stephanie*

Wear your life jacket out to the dock in the pond. ~ *Amy*

Don't go swimming without an adult. ~ *Danny*

Always do what you are supposed to do. ~ *Brooke*

Fourth Grade

Never hit a woman, even with the petal of a flower.
~ *Lydia (Phill's sister)*

Be kind and you will get kind back. ~ *Stephanie*

Tomorrow is a whole 'nother day. ~ *Alison*

Wash your hands before you eat. ~ *Peter, Lauren, Kim, & Angela*

Do your homework and you'll learn the truth. ~ *Stephanie*

Speak clearly. ~ *David & Nick*

Gramma taught me how to sew. ~ *Julia*

Gramma taught me how to draw. ~ *Michael*

f o u r t h   g r a d e

Never lean over the banister; remember Humpty Dumpty? ~ *Marcus*

You make me laugh! ~ *Ryan & Linda*

Keep your room clean! ~ *Andy & Angela*

Don't wear a coat, catch a cold. ~ *Nick*

You snooze, you lose! ~ *Geoff*

A problem is like a weed; it keeps growing. ~ *Jimmy*

Keep trying. ~ *Caitlin, Zach, Katie, & Emily*

Gramma taught me how to play cards & Crazy Eights!
~ *Lizzy, Laura, & Matt*

Always wear clean underwear;
you never know if you'll see a doctor. ~ *Matt*

Don't let your eyes get bigger than your stomach. ~ *David*

Be all that you can be! ~ *Erin*

Clean up after yourself! ~ *Matt & Ben*

Don't fight with your sister;
you never know when you'll need each other. ~ *Emily*

First, eat what's on your plate. ~ *Sarah*

Gramma taught me to talk nice. ~ *Matt*

Shut the door! Are you afraid your tail's gonna get caught? ~ *Erin*

Make good choices. ~ *Allie & Amanda*

Try to never talk back again. ~ *Mitch*

Never go out with your hair wet or you'll get sick. ~ *Luke*

If you put your mind to something, you can achieve it! ~ *Caitlin*

Don't pull on Santa's beard or you might not get presents. ~ *Staci*

Gramma taught me to wrap presents
the way she does. ~ *Chris*

Don't ever play with drugs. ~ *Jim & Chelsea*

Be nice to animals. ~ *Ryan*

Never ask the price of your birthday present. ~ *Andrew*

If I die I will still be with you. ~ *Jennifer*

If you can't fight nice, you shouldn't be fighting. ~ *Colleen*

A face without freckles is like a night without stars. ~ *Jake*

Always eat your vegetables. ~ *Katie & Lindsay*

Gramma taught me to make her famous spaghetti. ~ *Suzy*

Death is like birth. ~ *Pat*

Why put your mind to rest
when there is so much to think about? ~ *Mathew*

If you can't sleep, count sheep. ~ *Chris*

The world's gone mad! ~ *Jackie (Joey's sister)*

Smile a while and give your face a rest! ~ *Becky*

Gramma taught me to tie my shoe. ~ *Deanna*

Gramma taught me to play my first game. ~ *Mike*

If you love your relatives, spend time with them. *~ Lindsay*

Be responsible. *~ Kyle & Michael*

Don't get a tattoo. *~ Robert*

Don't cry over spilt milk, even if you spilt it. *~ James*

Don't make the basement such a mess! *~ David*

Write neatly. *~ Erica*

Gramma taught me how to cook and buy good towels.
~ Courtney & Marissa

One step at a time. ~ *Patty*

Don't watch too much TV. ~ *Betsy*

Love your family and friends. ~ *Matt*

Try your best. ~ *Deidre & Katie*

You're special and you should be proud of it. ~ *Alyssa*

Always remember your math. ~ *Jon*

Gramma taught me how to play tennis. ~ *Nick*

Gramma taught about Jesus and how to pray. ~ *Ryan & Eric*

When you go fishing, be quiet! ~ *Brandon*

Buy things on sale, save money. ~ *Sean*

Don't grow taller than your grandmother. ~ *Lisa*

Know what's going on around you. ~ *Kevin*

Let the sun shine down on you. ~ *Brittani*

Gramma taught me cheerleading cheers. ~ *Megan*

Gramma taught me to try new food. ~ *J.P.*

Lights out! ~ *Katie*

A penny found is a penny earned. ~ *Laura*

Gramma taught me not to play with matches. ~ *Erica*

Fifth Grade

Gramma's
House

Don't underestimate anyone. ~ *Chris*

If you want something, work for it. ~ *Brian*

Pray to God when you need help and courage
instead of trying to handle it yourself. ~ *Allison*

Lying will never get you anywhere. ~ *Chris*

For every action, there is a reaction. ~ *Alice*

A smiling face will get you places. ~ *Amanda*

Honesty is the best policy. ~ *Bryan*

Don't just sit there, do something. ~ *Chris*

Two wrongs don't make a right. ~ *Colleen & Laura*

Never hit a woman, not even with a petal of a flower.
~ *Phill (Lydia's brother)*

Don't walk away upset, just walk away. ~ *Kelly*

No crying in Gramma's house. ~ Joe

What do you know? Take a minute to tell me. ~ Robbie

Chew with your mouth closed. ~ *Melissa*

Money can't buy happiness. ~ *Melissa, Theresa, & Kendra*

If you're hungry, go eat worms. ~ *Meghan*

If there's a will, there's a way. ~ *Katie & Meghan*

Don't be mean to anyone if you wouldn't want
them to be mean to you. ~ *Nate & Chris*

Clean your room so you do not get hurt. ~ *Joey*

Good morning, Miss America. ~ Megan

Never be late. ~ *Kevin & Allison*

Weigh your words. ~ *Sam*

Always try your best. ~ *Ryan & Joe*

Take all you want, but eat all you take. ~ *Kim*

One mistake can turn into one beautiful masterpiece. ~ *Tim*

Dress warm or your toes will fall off. ~ *Mike*

Wash behind your ears. ~ *Brittany*

Be thankful for what you have. ~ *Michelle & Jacob*

Don't worry about it. ~ *Evan*

If you don't brush your teeth, bugs will grow. ~ *Rick*

Parsley always makes chicken noodle soup better. ~ *Mike*

Success and failure are less than a centimeter apart. ~ *Bryan*

Always clean your ears. ~ *Angie*

Always eat your vegetables. ~ *Jillian*

Weight broke the bridge down. ~ *Emily*

You don't peel apples. ~ *Matt*

Sit down before you hurt yourself. ~ *Erich*

Do homework before play. ~ *Christine, J.J., & Andy*

The world has gone mad. ~ *Joey (Jackie's brother)*

Hold onto your hat! Mama's at the wheel! ~ *Jessie*

You're a real loud boy. ~ *Ryan*

Don't forget to brush your teeth. ~ *Brent*

The acorn never falls far from the tree. ~ *Adam*

A woman's work is never done. ~ *Kristie*

Don't do that. You're going to hurt yourself. ~ *Katie*

If ifs and ands were pots and pans, there would be
no need for Tinker's dam. ~ *Anne*

Always eat your vegetables. ~ *Abbey*

Always put your underwear on
before you put your pants on. ~ *Jocelyn*

An apple a day keeps the doctor away. ~ *Dan*

It's better for the world to laugh with you
than the world to laugh at you. ~ *Katie*

Put a coat on or you'll catch a cold. ~ *Danny*

I wish I didn't have to buy lunch. ~ *Matt*

Let the smarty pants shine. ~ *David*

Don't jump in the house. ~ *Will*

Eat your carrots; they'll make your eyes strong. ~ *Desiree*

Go sit in the chair over there. ~ *Jimmy*

Keep it for college. ~ *Katherine*

Go put your coat on. ~ *Ali*

f i f t h   g r a d e

Follow God and we will all be reunited in heaven. ~ *Aaron*

Patience is needed while fishing. ~ *Chelsea*

Don't put too much flour in the chocolate donuts. ~ *Ashley*

Don't go to Columbus, Ohio, if you are for Michigan. ~ *Chase*

Sometimes you get the bear.
Sometimes the bear gets you. ~ *Lauren*

Homework first. ~ *Mike, Danny, Blake, & Stephanie*

Annihilate Ohio State and humble Woody Hayes. ~ *Bobby*

Believe in your guardian angel. You never know
when something will happen. ~ *Kelsey*

Don't swim until an hour after you eat. ~ *Megan*

Always try and get an "A." ~ *Krishna*

Your clothes don't match. ~ *Nicolette*

When you clean your room,
don't put your dirty clothes in your closet. ~ *Mike*

You are always my little worker. ~ *Aubrey*

Sixth Grade

If you need help, just ask for it. ~ *Angie*

Always work hard in school. ~ *David*

Snap snap, kids. ~ *Leah*

Always do your best. ~ *Megan*

Ask your grandpa. ~ *Chris*

It's never fun to get old. ~ *Anjali*

A watched pot never boils. ~ *Laura*

It's all going in the same place. ~ *Gabriella*

s i x t h   g r a d e

Never believe everything you hear. ~ *Mike*

Don't call your sister that. ~ *Sara*

No eats, no treats. ~ *Kristy*

Don't wake the baby. ~ *Allison*

You can do anything here, as long as it's safe. ~ *Sarah*

Always treat cards with respect. ~ *Jenny*

Have fun when you're young
because you're only young once. ~ *Todd*

Absence makes the heart grow fonder,
while peroxide makes the hair grow blonder. ~ *Betsy*

A spoonful of sugar helps the medicine go down. ~ *Ian*

Don't believe everything you read. ~ *Mike*

Always try to do better than the best. ~ *Chris*

That's good stuff. ~ *Ross*

Enjoy your childhood. ~ *Adam*

Losers weepers. ~ *Zach*

We have lots of pop. ~ *Jon*

Eat your food. ~ *Tim*

Good one, Simba. ~ *Megen*

Wait until after you eat to have gum. ~ *Michael*

Always read books; it makes you smarter. ~ *Kelly*

Be yourself, no matter what. ~ *Krista & Mike*

Put forth effort to all you do. ~ *Stacie*

Bad habits are hard to lose; try not to gain them. ~ *Nicole*

A family that prays together stays together. ~ *Erica*

Honesty is the best policy. ~ *Chrissy*

Always think before saying something. ~ *Nick*

Try hard in everything you do and don't give up. ~ *Jeff*

Learn something every day. ~ *Charlie*

Respect your elders. ~ *Haley*

Be nice to people. ~ *Danielle*

Actions speak better than words. ~ *Matt*

Life is short; play hard. ~ *Pete*

To make a friend is to be one. ~ *Nicole*

Success comes in cans, not can'ts. ~ *Brittany*

Life is like a gift; it's full of surprises. ~ *Stephen*

Always eat what your mother makes for dinner
even if it's gross. ~ *Lisa*

Respect the others around you. ~ *Arden*

Be proud when you do good things. ~ *Pat*

s i x t h   g r a d e

Knowledge is power. ~ *Pat*

Life is like sunshine. ~ *Erin*

Be a leader not a follower. ~ *Laura*

We can achieve our goals. ~ *Bryan*

Always give it 100 percent. ~ *Kelly*

Be kind to everyone, even people you don't know. ~ *Molly*

Always trust others. ~ *Jeffrey*

You can't have your cake and eat it too. ~ *Ben*

s i x t h   g r a d e

Go for it, never give up, and always do your best. ~ *Scott & Bryan*

Never trust another person's turn signal. ~ *Nate*

Take what God gives you and be happy. ~ *Monica*

Never waste anything that you can still use. ~ *Nick*

Have good manners. ~ *Jason & David*

Collect every penny you find
because it will amount to something one day. ~ *Jeff*

Become pope or president and impress the world. ~ *John*

Fishing isn't good with the wrong bait. ~ *Chris*

Wear a hat so you don't catch a cold. ~ *Jordan*

Try it; if you don't like it, it's okay. ~ *Jake*

Even if someone's mean to you, be nice to them. ~ *Amanda*

Never dress like a punk, or you will go to jail. ~ *Carly*

Don't throw anything away; give it to someone else. ~ *Lauren*

Go to church and be the best person you can be. ~ *Katelyn*

Remember, don't get into trouble. ~ *Andy*

Always go to church on Sunday
because you are Catholic. ~ *Christy*

Don't use money for things
that will rot your teeth and mind. ~ *Bryan*

Always try your best and never give up.
~ *Ryan, Brittany, & Amanda*

Be proud and thankful for who you are. ~ *Jenny*

Have a firm handshake.
People will think of you as a friendly person. ~ *Annie*

Say a Hail Mary when you're homesick,
or on a test. ~ *Jordan*

Gramma taught me how to make cookies. ~ *Katie*

Gramma taught me how to be patient. ~ *Christine*

Gramma taught me how to cure a bloody nose. ~ *Greg*

Seventh Grade

Don't give up. ~ *Mike*

Always buy food that is fat free. ~ *Karrie*

Stop making that face or it will freeze that way. ~ *Kevin*

Take your time and don't rush through things.
~ *Kristen & Emily*

Don't judge people on their looks
but by what is in their hearts. ~ *David*

Save your UPCs for rebates. You'll save! ~ *Mike*

Always wear clean clothes. ~ *Michelle*

What goes around, comes around. ~ *Mandy*

Don't do something today
that you can put off until tomorrow. ~ *Brian*

Always be a leader and not a follower. ~ *Kevin*

Keep your mouth closed when you chew. ~ *Amanda*

Keep your eye on the ball. ~ *Matt*

If you want to make a lot of money when you grow up,
learn to be a great golfer.
Ladies make a lot of money playing golf. ~ *Shelley*

Treat others the way you want to be treated. ~ *Katie*

Make sure you brush your teeth, both of them. ~ *Zac*

Be thankful for what you have. ~ *Megan*

If you stick your lip out when you're mad,
a bird might land on it. ~ *Jillian*

Don't eat too much or you will get sick. ~ *Christine*

Don't swim after you eat. ~ *Adam*

Always drink caffeine-free diet pop at night.
It's healthier for you and makes you sleep easier. ~ *Meghan*

s   e   v   e   n   t   h   g   r   a   d   e

Don't talk when other people are talking. ~ *Mark*

Always be nice. ~ *Joey*

Have fun in life. ~ *Josh*

Don't talk when Grandpa's on the phone. ~ *Lynn*

Don't sweat the little things. ~ *Carly*

If the sun is red in the morning, sailors take warning;
red at night, sailor's delight! ~ *Tom*

Chew your food forty times before you swallow. ~ *Jeff*

Grammas are made to spoil their grandchildren. ~ *Kelly*

A stitch in time saves nine. ~ *Michelle*

If you don't succeed, try and try again. ~ *Kris*

Drink your juice. ~ *Jon*

Always be good. ~ *Eric, Jim, & Greg*

Pray at least four times a day. ~ *Greg*

My father told me that my grandmother said,
"Never forget how you get to heaven." ~ *Amanda*

s e v e n t h g r a d e

If someone takes you out to dinner, order the lobster. ~ *David*

Always be polite. ~ *Jessica*

Don't drive a remote control car
into a puddle of water. ~ *Charlie*

Pray in your heart. ~ *Gina*

Put school before play. ~ *Chris*

Smile, child. ~ *Brittany*

(Whenever I say hey.) Save your hay,
you might marry a horse. ~ *Sarah*

Never just say you're fine.
You're probably not telling the whole truth. ~ *Meredith*

Live life to the fullest. ~ *Christopher*

Think before you act. ~ *Jaime*

Eat what you put on your plate. ~ *Katie*

Sports aren't as important as grades. ~ *Colin*

Be kind to those who you want to be kind back. ~ *Mike*

God is the most important thing in life.
And prayer too. ~ *Catie*

Love someone for what's on the inside,
not what's on the outside. ~ *Matt*

Just be sure you are happy. ~ *Ryan*

You can't cry at my house unless you are bleeding. ~ *Katie*

Don't eat a lot of candy. ~ *Leah*

Make things go your way. ~ *Andrea*

Never grow taller than your gramma. ~ *Marjorie*

You can't miss a place if you've never been there. ~ *Nicole*

Never be too busy to call your gramma. ~ *Angela*

Always add a little bit of this and a little bit of that
to make a tasty recipe. ~ *Ali*

Be kind to everyone, even if they're unkind to you.
~ *Jessie & Renee*

Don't count your chickens before they hatch. ~ *Steve*

You're never too old to go to Disneyland. ~ *Monica*

Know your priorities in life. ~ *Katy*

Always get nine hours of sleep. ~ *Erik*

Dress in heavy layers when it's cold outside. ~ *Michael*

Look on the bright side of things. ~ *Megan*

Think before you speak. ~ *Chad*

Don't take things too seriously. ~ *Chris*

Not everybody is going to like you. ~ *Alex*

Don't play with fire. ~ *Lee*

Learn how to make chocolate chip cookies. ~ *Katie*

Always check the local garage sales. ~ *Katie*

It doesn't matter what others think,
just be yourself. ~ *Megan & Amanda*

Don't talk to strangers. ~ *Andrew & Julie*

Take a shower every day. ~ *Frank*

Give your all. ~ *Adam*

Give 110 percent. ~ *Chris*

Life is as fun as you make it. ~ *Dan*

Never say never. ~ *Phil*

Eighth Grade

If you have to misbehave, do it at home. *~ Sally*

Don't be a leader or a follower; be a friend. *~ Meridith*

Look both ways before you cross the street.
~ Jonah, Jennifer, & Adam

If you can't say something nice,
then don't say anything at all. *~ Chris & Joe*

An apple a day keeps the doctor away. *~ Kristyn*

A watched pot never boils. *~ Kelly*

e   i   g   h   t   h   g   r   a   d   e

Home is where the heart is. ~ *Jessica*

Good things come in small packages. ~ *Dave*

Eat your vegetables. ~ *Amanda*

A penny saved is a penny earned. ~ *Adam*

Always do your homework. ~ *Charlie & Kevin*

Try harder the second time. ~ *Jon*

Don't be afraid to laugh at a joke even if it's stupid. ~ *Erich*

Help when help is needed. ~ *Seann*

Don't let anyone tell you who you are. ~ *Elizabeth*

Never let anyone tell you that you can't do it. ~ *Natalie*

Brush your teeth three times a day. ~ *Kate*

Never call a gramma, Gramma. ~ *Casidy*

It's the thought that counts. ~ *Joe*

Don't play with matches. ~ *Bobby*

Golly! ~ *Lindsay*

Love is the best medicine for any ache or pain. ~ *Mary*

Don't play on the railroad tracks
when the train is coming. ~ *Rob*

The grass is always greener on the other side. ~ *Alan & Paul*

Don't count your chickens before they hatch. ~ *Brian*

Study hard, get good grades,
and you can have steak every night. ~ *Becca*

Wherever you go, you'll always have a friend. ~ *Andrew*

Never judge a book by its cover. ~ *Rory*

If you can't take the heat, get out of the kitchen. ~ *Margaret*

He seems like a nice boy. ~ *Callie*

If you can't say something nice, don't say anything at all.
~ *Joe, Amy, Mike, & Jordan*

Just be yourself. ~ *Laura*

If you think you can, you can.
If you think you can't, you're right. ~ *Sarah*

Kill them with kindness. ~ *Susie & Anne*

Always try your hardest. ~ *Peter, Tim, & Chris*

Don't jump on the bandwagon. ~ *Chris*

Holy Moly! ~ *Matt*

Stay away from those boys! ~ *Stephanie*

Shut the door; you're letting the heat out! ~ *Jon*

Keep an open mind. ~ *Chad*

Be happy. ~ *Bryan*

It will work out in the end. ~ *Nick*

When you live under my roof... ~ *Matt*

e i g h t h   g r a d e

Follow your dreams. ~ *Kristen & Julie*

You'll always be my little monster. ~ *Andrea*

If Mom says no, ask Gramma or Grandpa. ~ *Danielle, Joe, & Mike*

Never date an older woman. ~ *Matt*

When the Lord shuts a door, He opens a window. ~ *Mary*

Would you like some salad on your dressing? ~ *John*

Good food always makes one feel better. ~ *Nikki*

Grammas give love. ~ *Casey*

e   i   g   h   t   h   g   r   a   d   e

Keep your head to the stars and your feet on the ground. ~ *Lauren*

When I was your age, I had to walk five miles to school, uphill, both ways, in twenty feet of snow! We didn't have buses. ~ *Joe & Natalie*

Don't say words you can't spell. ~ *Anne & Mary*

Never go swimming after dinner. ~ *Nicole & Caitlin*

Eat your dinner. ~ *Adam, Matt, & Nicole*

Eat your broccoli. Some children somewhere would love to have this. ~ *Matt*

Your Favorite Gramma-isms

Your Favorite Gramma-isms

by Rick Luettke

About the Authors

Sally Koppinger and Libbey Koppinger, mother and daughter, come from a family of artists, teachers, thinkers, craftsmen, and all-around hard workers.

Sally is the principal of St. Joseph School in Sylvania, Ohio. She has worked in education as a teacher and principal for the last twenty years, and lives in Toledo, Ohio, with her husband of thirty-three years, Nicholas.

Libbey, author of *Legacy: Gifts from a Grandmother,* is an art director. She and her husband, Larry, are expecting their first child in March 1998.

More Legacies *Books and Gifts from Papier-Mache Press*

Book
Legacy: Gifts from a Grandmother
by Libbey Koppinger
More valuable than any family heirloom, the words of our grandmothers are truly a legacy to be treasured and remembered. This delightful collection of "gramma-isms" will bring an instant smile and warm memories of caring hugs and home-baked cookies.
ISBN 0-918949-68-8, trade paper

Gifts
Gramma Mug and Apron Set
Colorful apons are rolled up and tucked into two matching mugs, bagged in see-through cellophane, and ribbon-tied with a copy of *Legacy*.
GRA5132

Love Is... Mug
"Love Is What You Do Not What You Say" in blue and green design on white mug.
GRA0311

Make Time... Mug
"Make Time for Yourself" in blue and green design on white mug.
GRA0312

Gramma Apron
Cheerful full-color design on white apron for adults.
GRA0102

Gramma Child's Apron
Cheerful full-color design on white apron for kids.
GRA0102C

Gramma Poster
Full-color poster with 8x10 mat.
GRA0291

Gramma Poster
Full-color poster with 11x14 mat.
GRA0292

Papier-Mache Press

At Papier-Mache Press, it is our goal to identify and successfully present important social issues through enduring works of beauty, grace, and strength. Through our work we hope to encourage empathy, respect, and communication among all people—young and old, male and female.

We offer many beautiful books and gift items. Please ask your local bookstore or gift store which Papier-Mache items they carry. To obtain our complete catalog, mail your request to Papier-Mache Press, 627 Walker Street, Watsonville, CA 95076; call our toll-free number, 800-927-5913; or e-mail your request to papierma@sprynet.com. You can also browse our complete catalog on the web at http://www.ReadersNdex.com/papiermache.